CRYSTAL WORKBOOK

Crystal Workbook

Sheril Berkovitch

GEMCRAFT BOOKS

Revised 1995 edition published by
Gemcraft Books
14 Duffy Street Burwood
Victoria 3125 Australia

Reprinted November 1995
First published in 1992
by Labrys

Printed in Australia
by McPherson's Printing Group

Cover Photo: The Face in the Crystal.
A miraculous natural crystal of Brazilian quartz with amazing inclusions.
The crystal measures 12 cm by 6 cm.

National Library of Australia
Cataloguing-in-publication entry

Berkovitch, Sheril.
  Crystal workbook.

  Bibliography.
  ISBN 0 909223 97 1.

  1. Crystals – Therapeutic use. 2. Precious stones –
  Therapeutic use. 3. Chakras. I. Title

131

This book is a reference work based on the research and experience of the author. The opinions expressed are not necessarily those of the publisher. The information in this book is in no way intended to replace consultation with a licensed wholistic physician.

Contents

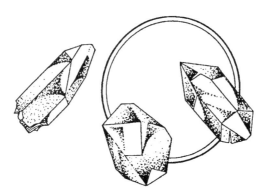

Introduction

This book is the result of many months at the computer with piles of books, my own notes, and hours of sitting with crystals and healing stones and reading them. The idea for the book came initially through the many people who visit our crystal shop, wanting a ready reference to the healing properties of crystals and stones. I decided to gather together as much information as I could on those stones that are more easily found, and those that I have had the pleasure to work with, spend some time with and get to know.

Of course, what you have before you is not the definitive dictionary of crystals and healing stones. There isn't one. Every day, as I work with, collect and hold different crystals and healing stones, I find out something new about them. What I have collected here are snippets of the vast banks of material available from previous writers and channels, and information given to me by the stones themselves.

Quite often, when I am working with a stone and/or a chakra, I realise that the stone can be used for a particular purpose or goal. When people come into our shop and ask for particular stones for particular chakras, I often tell them that although the colour of the stone may correspond to a certain chakra point, it might be just as useful held in the hand, kept in a pocket or around the neck, or on your bedside cabinet. As you get to know your stones, you will discover their best use for you.

This book doesn't even try to give you detailed information on how to use crystals and healing stones. This is another book! Meanwhile, you can source this information elsewhere through other books, workshops, seminars, or by simply holding the crystals and stones in your hand and using them. I have found Katrina Raphael's books most useful in this respect, along with workshops and seminars with Trisha Ellis from the Crystal Academy in South Australia and Barbara Buchanan, who works in Melbourne. Workshops and courses have been most beneficial because they not only give information about the healing properties of crystals and stones, but also give much needed hands-on experience before venturing into the world of healing.

You may find that you'll make changes to the way you work once you have some hands-on experience of working with crystals and healing stones; you will adapt what you learn from others to suit yourself. I always tell my clients and customers, there is no wrong way of using healing stones - whatever works for you and resonates with you is the right way for you.

Sheril Berkovitch

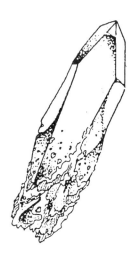

CleansinG CRysTals and HealinG STones

There are many methods used by different crystal workers for cleansing and clearing their crystals and healing stones. These are the various methods I use.

Cleansing Your Stones Under Running Water

Make sure the water is not too hot or too cold, so that any natural cracks in the stone are not exacerbated by the effect of the water. If you live near a river or stream, all well and good, but otherwise tepid tap water will be just as good. Hold your stone under the water for a few minutes, and while concentrating on its energy, ask for all negative and unharmonious vibrations and energies to leave and only those that are beneficial and positive to stay. Gently dry your stone with a cotton towel. It is then ready to use.

Smudging With Incense

Some healing stones such as calcite, selenite and dioptase will crumble or cleave on contact with water. With these stones, use incense for cleansing. Sage and cedar (used by native Americans) and sandalwood are the best, because they are cleansing substances, although any sandalwood-based incense will suffice. Surround your stone with the cleansing smoke of a smudge stick or incense stick, while asking for it to be cleansed of any negative or unharmonious vibrations and energies.

Placing on a Cluster

One easy way of cleansing your stones is to place them on an amethyst or clear quartz cluster. They can use the cluster as their permanent home. Amethyst in particular has cleansing properties. Clear quartz clusters will assist your stone in building up its healing energies.

The Sun and the Moon

Crystals and healing stones enjoy sitting in the sunlight and moonlight. They will be rejuvenated and cleansed. Remember to keep water-sensitive stones out of the rain. You may wish to place them in a window which receives much sunlight or moonlight.

Burying in the Ground

Bury your stone a couple of inches below the ground, remembering where it is! A terminated crystal should be placed with the point down. Visualise cleansing and healing energy going into the stone. After 24 hours, unearth your stone. If it feels as if it needs more time, rebury it, keeping an eye on it until it is ready to come out and be used for healing work. This is a good method for stones that you haven't managed to cleanse and clear with either the water or smudging methods. (Don't use this method for water-sensitive stones in case of rain!)

The Crystals and Stones

There are countless crystals, gems and minerals, and they can all be used for healing. The following list is just a few in the mountain of possibilities, and I hope to add to it over time.

The crystals and stones are listed in alphabetical order.

Enjoy!

AGATE

Agate is a banded microcrystalline quartz. It is often found with other quartz minerals such as amethyst and carnelian.

Chakra: According to stone colour.

Agates are very powerful healing stones. They are grounding but also build up energy. They will tone and strengthen the link between body and mind, imparting a sense of strength and courage and enhancing the ability to discern truth and accept circumstances. They are balancing and stabilising to all bodies.

Be careful of brightly coloured blue and green agates, as they have generally been dyed, and often their natural energies will have dissipated or died.

Botswana Agate

Use both the grey and pink varieties at the heart chakra. It will assist in calming the heart and grounding the heart energies into the physical body. Enhances creativity and imparts a strength of character and understanding. Use for opening the crown chakra. Helps maintain concentration and attentiveness. Use to help clear the body of toxins, especially those left behind by the use of drugs. Excellent to help those recovering from addictions.

Crazy Lace Agate

The various shades of grey, brown and red make crazy lace

agate most useful for grounding and energising the base/root chakra. Helps raise physical energy.

Dendritic Agate

This helps maintain equilibrium and ensures that energy is directed in the areas where it is most needed.

Fire Agate

Assists in lifting lethargy. Strengthens physical vitality, cuts through sluggishness and helps focus on the present. Assists in circulatory and nervous system disorders. Helps clear blocks on the emotional and physical bodies. Brings clarity and understanding to all situations. (Brown to black with orange and red tints.) Root chakra.

Tree Agate

When used at the crown chakra, tree agate will help to slow down fast-moving energies that the mental body cannot handle. It is less grounding than other agates. Tree agate is a good companion at the heart chakra for soothing emotional pain.

Moss Agate

Heart chakra. Powerful physical healer, especially for heart and lung dis-ease. Works on the emotional and mental patterns that manifest dis-ease, helping to clear those patterns and regenerate tissues. A good stone for people with cancer to assist in recognising negative patterns that are eating away at them. A link to the plant and mineral kingdoms, assisting in communicating with the natural world and nature spirits. Excellent as an elixir for skin disorders.

ALEXANDRITE

Alexandrite, a variety of chrysoberyl, is an extremely rare

stone which changes colour according to the light, from greenish to deep purple and red. Because of its rarity, it is very expensive, so most alexandrites on the market have been grown in laboratories rather than naturally over thousands of years.

Chakra: Crown

Alexandrite is a regenerative stone, aiding the tissues of the body to renew after dis-ease - both internally and externally. It reacts positively on the nervous system, spleen and pancreas. Its regenerative properties also apply to spiritual transformation and growth. It helps to align the emotional and mental bodies. It enhances your ability to find joy in life. Its changing colour signifies a spiritual metamorphosis and it is therefore an excellent stone for 'newcomers' to spiritual growth. Alexandrite has the ability to impart the blue, red, purple/violet and green colour rays. Also an excellent stone for psychic protection. Assists in regeneration and rebirth, particularly on the spiritual level. Its corresponding organs are the spleen, pancreas and nervous system. Has been used to treat leukaemia and cancer.

AMAZONITE

Amazonite is an opaque, blue-green feldspar.

Chakra: Throat

Can be held in meditation to take you beyond your physical self. Helps alleviate the fear of out-of-body experiences. Strengthens heart and physical body. Excellent for enhancing creative expression and gives a clear vision of your harmful tendencies, making them easier to release. Amazonite can be useful for someone who is terminally ill - having it in the room can benefit their transition. Provides a sense of continuity and understanding between body and spirit. Beneficial for opening the throat chakra to receive the healing energies of the blue ray. Soothing to the nervous system, and excellent for building confidence and self-esteem and a belief in oneself. Aligns the physical, astral and etheric bodies, making astral travel easier and the coming back smoother. Balances male and female energies.

AMBER

Amber is the fossilised resin of pine trees, formed fifty to seventy million years ago. It ranges in colour from light yellow to golden brown, and often has inclusions of insects, parts of plants, carbon deposits or air bubbles.

Chakra: Navel/Sexual, Solar Plexus

Amber has uplifting energies, and is especially helpful when you are feeling weighed down with responsibilities. It is good for people with suicidal tendencies and those who easily get depressed. Helps you find humour and joy. Creates a balance between daily life and spiritual expansion. Utilise amber when you are feeling powerless or out of control, to remind you of your inner strength and past achievements. Amber has a positive effect on the endocrine system, spleen and heart, and has a healing, soothing, harmonising influence.

Amber revitalises the internal organs when used for healing. Worn as jewellery, it can be grounding and stabilising. When used at the solar plexus, amber will enhance intellectual clarity about your future path. Absorbs toxins from the environment.

AMETHYST

A member of the quartz family. Ranges in colour from light lavender, through violet to almost black. Australian amethyst is particularly dark.

Chakra: Third Eye or Crown

Amethyst enhances right-brain activity. It is a blood cleanser and energiser. Assists purification and regeneration, and cuts through illusion.

Amethyst has a calming mental effect, and is one of the best stones to use for meditation. Use for overworked, overstressed and overwhelmed mental states. Especially good for people suffering from recurrent nightmares. Amethyst will help clear and transform energies in the environment where it is placed, and will help to release unbalanced energies. Also helps you understand your dreams.

Amethyst has strong protective qualities and will enhance psychic abilities and spiritual awareness. Balances and soothes an over-active mind.

Mythology says that amethyst helps us remain sober; it is the stone that Bacchus used to cure his drunkenness.

Amethyst can also be utilised for cleansing other crystals and stones, by placing them on an amethyst cluster.

The endocrine and immune system can be strengthened by amethyst, and it is useful in the treatment of emotional/mental disorders, nervous disorders and easing pain. As an elixir it is useful for easing the pain of arthritis.

AMETRINE

A combination of amethyst and citrine which occurs when amethyst is naturally heated in the ground or natural environment. *Chakras:* Solar Plexus, Third Eye and Crown.

Ametrine combines the energies and properties of amethyst and citrine, and is a stone of transformation and change, signified by its changing colour.

It clears blocks at the solar plexus, particularly those related to fear of the unknown and fear of change. Ametrine provides for clearer insight into your reason for being and ease of decision making. It is an excellent meditation stone that will assist you in going deeper and clarifying issues and problems. Ametrine will also assist in making meditation more productive.

Relieves stress and tension and provides a calming effect. A good stone to use in long-term work in developing spiritually and psychically. A friend.

ANGELITE

Also known as massive anhydrite. Light blue in colour, dense and milky on occasions.

Chakra: Throat or Heart

Angelite soothes fear, anxiety and trauma, and imparts a feeling of well-being and satisfaction. It builds acceptance of the struggles ahead and enhances the ability to cope with them.

Excellent for creative people, artists and craftspersons, enhances self-expression and your ability to communicate clearly. Helps you to be realistic and objective about problems. Quiets an over-active mind.

Angelite influences the bones, nervous system and brain. Use it at the heart or throat chakra for linking the heart and throat energies for self-expression and the verbalising of your heart's desire. A useful stone for people who have trouble expressing what they want. Angelite also contains the soothing and calming energies of water - you go with the flow. Imparts a carefree feeling. Beneficially influences the thyroid. An excellent stone for people who do a lot of public speaking. Use with blue calcite for clarity of expression.

This stone is excellent for those learning a new language, or for those who sing. It helps the voice to be clear and soothes a sore throat. Angelite can be used to place a protective force-field around people and things. Enhances telepathy and dispels anger. An excellent stone for psychic healers.

APATITE

Apatite can be colourless, pink, yellow, green, blue and violet. It is most often found in crystal form with multiple faces, although sometimes it can be found in massive form.

Chakra: According to stone colour.

Yellow and Yellow/Green Apatite: Solar Plexus and Heart Chakra

A stellar-beam crystal which will enhance other world connections. A soul connector. A very spacy stone, which will create much mental activity.

Apatite is comforting, inward looking and creative. It is excellent for meditation and for holding when you feel worried. Will assist in clarifying issues and problems when you are not sure what to do. Enhances the ability to show unconditional love towards others and also enhances self-empowerment and self-esteem.

Aids in the manifestation of your heart's desire. Strengthens the pineal and pituitary glands.

Blue Apatite: Throat Chakra

Enhances your ability to communicate with extra-terrestrial beings. Enhances creative expression, and especially good for artists, writers and musicians working to create love and well-being through their work. Heightens perception and understanding and the ability to communicate your ideas and needs. Works very much on the emotional and spiritual levels. Corresponding organs are the thyroid, heart, ears and eyes.

APOPHYLLITE

Clear or green crystal, most commonly found in Poona, India. Green is much rarer.

Chakra: All chakras, but especially the Crown for clear, and the Heart for green.

Clear Apophyllite

This crystal enhances clarity of mind and enables you to let go of old patterns. It is uplifting and cheerful. Helps in contacting your guides and teachers. A link to past lives. Beneficial to many organs, but especially the heart, adrenal glands, spleen and brain. Stimulates intuition and raises energy levels.

Green Apophyllite

When you are making big changes in your life, especially in the development of your spiritual path, green apophyllite will help you on your journey. Balances the heart chakra. Helps you communicate with nature and the environment. Calming for the mind and emotionally balancing. A soft and gentle stone. Activates the heart chakra. Corresponding organs are the heart, muscles, spleen and brain.

AQUAMARINE

Light blue to blue and sometimes slightly greenish, translucent crystal; a member of the beryl family.

Chakra: Throat

Helps you find deeper satisfaction when you are feeling discouraged or empty. Teaches you to value yourself and others. Reassuring, uplifting, points towards spiritual fulfilment.

Aquamarine enhances clarity of mind and has a beneficial effect on the kidneys, liver, spleen and thyroid. It is a purifying stone and an excellent balancer on all levels. Aquamarine is good for assisting in banishing fears and phobias and imparts feelings of inspiration, calmness, peace and love. Helps in situations where you need to be in control.

This gemstone shields the aura from negative vibrations, and can temporarily protect you from pollution. Its energy is that of water, flowing but strong, gentle and compassionate. It activates and cleanses the throat chakra. Excellent for treating glandular problems and disorders of the eyes.

ARAGONITE

White, brown, yellow, purplish or reddish in colour. Twinned hexagonal crystals.

Chakra: According to stone colour.

Aragonite balances the male and female aspects of character. It also balances the emotions, especially of those who are over-emotional or overly blocked. A very calming and nurturing crystal which enhances sensitivity and creativity, and gives you the ability to give and receive with comfort. Enhances intellectual clarity and perception. Beneficial for the nervous system, heart and brain. An excellent meditation stone. Stimulates communication and insight.

AVENTURINE

This stone is usually green with sparkly inclusions of hematite or mica. It is a member of the quartz family. Peach and blue aventurine are now also available. (Peach aventurine is sometimes referred to as red or orange aventurine.)

Chakras: According to stone colour. Green corresponds to the heart, blue to the third eye and peach to the solar plexus, navel or heart chakras.

Green Aventurine

Aids in releasing anxiety and fear. Stimulates muscle tissue, strengthens blood. Independence, health and well-being are enhanced by using this stone.

Green aventurine will help you move on from a limited vision of your capabilities. It encourages exploration and creativity in many ways, and is helpful in career assessment and changes. Assists in bringing in feelings of emotional tranquillity and a positive attitude towards life. A good stone to carry or wear in times of emotional turmoil and stress to assist in balancing. An all-round healer.

Blue Aventurine

Helps you to see the way forward more clearly in all aspects of your life, and helps solve problems. However, do not rely too closely on this stone for 'answers', for what it will do is show you what choices are available. It is up to you to make the final decision.

Blue aventurine will assist in breaking down belief systems that prevent you from taking the most beneficial path. Imparts a sense of belief in yourself and your ability to make correct decisions.

It is advantageous to use blue aventurine when exploring options for careers, relationships and future foundations. Its energies are very focused and constant. It can be a very good friend in difficult times.

Peach Aventurine

A good companion to the regenerative and rejuvenative energies of carnelian. Peach aventurine works on the physical body to help heal damaged muscle tissue. A good stone to use following childbirth to strengthen the muscles. Peach aventurine will help you in following your gut feelings about the future, particularly in relation to spiritual matters. Use with blue aventurine and green aventurine when decisions need to be made to calm and still the mind and heart.

AZURITE

Deep (royal) blue. Takes the form of a dense aggregate, small crystals or spherical balls. Often occurs with malachite and/or chrysocolla near copper deposits.

Chakra: Third Eye

The energies of change and purification. Increases intuitiveness and sensitivity. Steady inward focus. Good stones for meditation to help clear and balance the third eye so it can receive finer energies.

Azurite initiates transformation and is good to use with other transformational stones related to the third eye. It facilitates clear meditation and will help cleanse the mental body, thereby assisting clarity. Encourages the process of renewal by assisting mental patterns to surface so they can be reviewed. Enhances communication with others and the ability to listen. Use at the third eye when you are having problems seeing clearly. Enhances creativity, intuition and psychic ability. Excellent for use in meditation to enhance the relaxed state.

Azurite-Malachite combination

When used at the third eye, the azurite-malachite combination stone will strengthen the abilities of azurite alone, bringing more clarity, understanding and clearer vision.

BARITE

Brown, yellow, blue, green, gold or colourless crystals, usually found on their matrix rock.

Chakra: According to stone colour.

Barite will help clear blocked energies, particularly those related to emotional trauma. It has the ability to draw you out of feeling sorry for yourself into a more positive framework.

Green barite can be used at the heart chakra for bringing up, clearing and releasing entities or past-life memories that are preventing you from moving on in the present. Helps clear emotional blocks. Beneficial to the bones and especially useful for calcium retention in women.

Brown Barite

Base Chakra. Clears subconscious blocks to enable the opening of the base chakra to the earth's healing energies. Brown barite can work very quickly to dissolve feelings of disquiet and concern about situations that are not of your doing. Its message is live and let live. Clears unwanted and lingering negative energies, releases feelings of nervousness and fear, and soothes old anger. Beneficial to the bladder. Helps heal the appendix.

Green Barite

Heart Chakra. Works with the subtle bodies to release stored anger and resentment. Clears trapped energies such as entities that are eating away at you. Very seldom works directly on physical ailments, preferring to go straight to the source. Excellent for aura cleansing. Generally an emotional balancer and rejuvenator. A good companion at the heart is green or pink calcite which will provide more soothing energies for barite's purging effect. Don't be surprised if you feel like crying when holding barite. It could be just the release you need at that time.

BLOODSTONE

Also sometimes known as heliotrope. Opaque, dark green chalcedony speckled with red jasper.

Chakra: Root or Heart

Assists in realigning spiritual purpose through clearing self-doubt. Gives strength and stamina during periods of stress, difficulty and loss of hope. Aids in clearing feelings of weakness. Helps calm scattered thoughts in preparation for meditation.

Bloodstone is a powerful physical healer, particularly good for use in dis-ease related to emotional stress. It assists inner guidance and is a link between the root and heart chakras. It strengthens and oxygenates the bloodstream. A powerful cleanser and healer for the physical body. Assists in regeneration and enhances creativity. Bloodstone can be useful to help you make decisions.

BLUE LACE AGATE

Light blue, banded quartz. It is usually available as tumbled stones or cabochons.

Chakra: Throat

Blue lace agate helps to open and expand consciousness. Enhances creativity and confident expression. Calming to the mind, soothing to the emotions. Encourages communication, wisdom, patience, peace, kindness and honesty. It influences the thyroid and nervous system. Strengthens a sense of calm centredness to help in social situations. Discourages nervous habits. Useful for building confidence in public speaking. It is also excellent for cooling hot tempers and relieving stress. This stone can be carried or worn when you want to maintain calm. Good for neutralising energies such as anger, infection, inflammation and fever. Blue lace agate opens the throat chakra for other stones to be used to express higher wisdom.

BOJI STONE
Concretions of pyrite surrounding (usually) a fossilised sea shell. The 'male' bojis are bumpy, while the 'female' are smooth.
Chakras: All
Highly energetic but also grounding. Joyful, happy stones. Carry them around in pairs; they will impart a sense of joy in your existence. A link to mother nature.

Boji stones are excellent for past-life work and the removal of energy blocks. Their electromagnetic energy field assists in drawing out pain and transferring energy from the etheric body to the physical. A pair of male and female stones provides balance on all levels. Use for tissue regeneration, strengthening the immune system and improving blood circulation.

CALCITE
Found in many colours. There are some 700 varieties of calcite.
Chakra: According to stone colour.

Green Calcite: Heart Chakra
Erases reverberations of shock. Promotes a peaceful sense of being in control of life. Balances and calms. Helps calm nervous

stomach and nervousness in general. Soothing, gentle energy. Helps release old mental patterns. A healer and friend in times of transition and readjustment, and mental changes. Good for rheumatic illness, arthritis and injuries involving bone and ligament damage. Aids healing following toxic fume inhalation or allergies to toxic chemicals.

Blue Calcite: Throat Chakra

Helps balance and calm emotional and mental levels, enabling you to see clearly what action you might take. Use when overwhelmed with the intensity of change. Lessens the sense of trauma and helps you move more easily through changes. Assists with the expression of emotions.

Honey Calcite: Solar Plexus Chakra

When doing a body layout, honey calcite is a good stone to give your client to hold in the right hand. Helps lift energies in difficult situations. Helpful during intense periods of change. Alleviates tiredness, burdens, or feelings of disillusionment. Honey calcite is also a calming stone.

Clear (Icelandic) Calcite: All Chakras, particularly the Crown.

Clear calcite alleviates fear and reduces stress. Like all calcites, it is an emotional balancer and very calming. Use in meditation to help ground excess energies and increase the capacity for astral projection. Joyful and light-hearted. Enhances spiritual awareness and gives a feeling of connectedness and well-being.

Gold Calcite: Navel or Crown Chakra

Good for meditation. Wear or carry gold calcite when you need to be mentally alert. When used at the crown chakra, it will assist in channelling the highest mental faculties into the physical body for manifestation. Enhances clarity of thought and vision and the ability to see the truth.

Pink and Peach Calcite: Heart Chakra
Helps heal the heart of emotional pain and trauma. Soothing and calming. Has a very uplifting energy.

Stellar Beam Calcite: Crown Chakra
Also known as dogtooth calcite. Opens the crown chakra to bring in pure white light. Enhances spiritual awareness and provides a feeling of protection.

Red Calcite: Base/Root or Solar Plexus Chakra
Provides a safe, grounded space for you to open up emotionally. Absorbs negative emotions that are blocking and unbalancing the lower chakras.

CARNELIAN

Orange red to orange brown in colour or shades of deep gold; a variety of chalcedony. Natural carnelian has a cloudy distribution of colour. Sometimes known as cornelian.

Chakra: Navel, Solar Plexus

A purifier, particularly for the physical body. Calming and centering. An excellent stone to help ease the trauma of abuse.

Orange/Red/Brown Carnelian

These are very highly evolved mineral healers. They energise the blood, aid kidneys, lungs, liver, gall bladder and help tissue regeneration. Vitalise physical, emotional and mental bodies. Warming, joyous. They serve as a grounder of energies and manifester on the physical plane. Good for people who are absent-minded, confused and unfocused. Aid concentration. Stimulate a deeper love and appreciation for the beauty and gifts of the earth. Aid optimism, and enable you to act more spontaneously. Lift gloom and despondency, sooth irritation. Assist in past-life exploration.

Yellow Carnelian

This stone has a more gentle, refined vibration than orange carnelian. It continues the process begun by that stone and helps you enjoy the journey. Imparts a feeling of optimism.

CASSITERITE

This is the principal ore of tin, so cassiterite crystals are tin crystals. Dark brown, almost black in colour, but sometimes with golden-brown highlights and rainbow inclusions.

Chakra: Base

An excellent energy conductor. Use at the base chakra for grounding, and for directing the upper chakra energies through to the lower chakras. Cassiterite acts like a magnet for these energies.

Cassiterite crystals with rainbows enhance the feeling of the joy of life. They build energy when you need endurance, therefore an excellent stone for those who engage in sports or daily physical work. Used at the solar plexus, the lighter crystals with a golden colour bring a feeling of warmth and contentedness with life's path.

A stone which is very oriented towards physical healing, although it will also be beneficial in time to come for aura healing work. Currently it is still evolving its healing energies, but at present it will serve those who operate on a mostly physical level very well.

Cassiterite is an excellent healer for women who have experienced surgery to the reproductive system. It soothes the pain of wounds such as cuts, bruises and sprains. Cassiterite can be used for the treatment of hormonal imbalance, such as menopause.

CELESTITE

Light blue, found often in clusters on sedimentary rock. Also found in transparent white crystal spears.

Chakra: Throat, Third Eye, or Crown for clear celestite.

Celestite helps clear left-brain clutter so you can connect with your higher being. Calming, relaxing. Empties the mind for rest and relaxation or meditation. Eases doubts grown in the rational mind. It aids personal creative expression, accelerates growth, particularly spiritual, and enhances clear speech or expression. Helps you adjust to higher states of awareness. Assists in contacting spirit guides and gives access to ancient records. A manifestation and astral traveller's stone. Enhances thyroid functions.

CERUSSITE

Crystallises in the form of masses, grains, stalactites, clusters and single crystals. Cerussite is an important ore of lead.

Chakra: Crown

Relieves tension and anxiety and soothes nervous/tense headaches. Encourages spiritual growth. Use cerussite to develop your capacity to listen to yourself and others, enhance creativity and co-operation, and to improve past-life recall. Assists sleep and imparts a mental calmness. Aligns the nervous system. Promotes spiritual growth and assists in developing a less introspective character. Grounding and comforting.

CHALCEDONY (White)

A variety of quartz. It is porous and therefore often dyed. Natural white chalcedony has no layering or banding.

Chakra: Solar Plexus, Navel

Chalcedony encourages the expression of emotional needs. It brings calmness and peace. Promotes emotional honesty and the expression of feelings that you tend to smother. Assists when moving through times of sadness and regret. An emotional balancer, energiser and soother. Alleviates anger and irritability. Enhances mental stability.

CHAROITE

Appears in the form of masses and tiny crystal druse on host rock. Its colour ranges from a brilliant purple, through to duller purple and pink to purple.

Chakra: Third Eye

Charoite is one of the most highly evolved mineral healers of the purple ray. It accelerates spiritual growth and transformation. Charoite assists in clearing emotional and mental blocks which prevent you changing your attitude, and it will help alleviate negative emotions such as fear and anger.

If you are resisting change, charoite will help break through the barriers. Enhances self-esteem, intuition, and assists in bringing about a relaxing, meditative state. Excellent for those recuperating from dis-ease, particularly from surgery.

Charoite enhances your ability to be loving and generous. It is beneficial to many organs, but especially the nervous system, pituitary gland and kidneys.

This stone assists in breathing disorders such as asthma and bronchitis, and it can be used in alleviating problems of the eyes and heart, and to help ease aches and pains, particularly headaches.

CHIASTOLITE

Appears in the form of wand-shaped massive crystals which, when polished, show cross shapes.

Chakra: Navel

An excellent stone for those leaving this physical plane (or passing over). Chiastolite will assist in making a smooth transition. Aids insight and problem solving.

CHRYSOCOLLA

Opaque, blue-green hydrous copper silicate. Often found with malachite and/or azurite, rarely with dioptase. Australian chrysocolla tends to be dark blue-green. Often occurs with cuprite. See also Gem Silica (quartz-infused chrysocolla).

Chakra: Throat, Heart, Third Eye

Chrysocolla helps clarify your spiritual purpose by alleviating the fear of expression. It also helps clear links with the past as you move forward. Enhances creative expression, power and communication. Helps prevent dis-ease caused by stress such as ulcers, digestive problems and arthritis.

This stone is an activator of feminine qualities. It is used by women to alleviate situations such as menstrual irregularity and the birthing process. Useful for men wishing to seek out their feminine aspects.

Chrysocolla provides a link to Mother Earth both physically and spiritually. Relieves distress caused by negative emotions. Enhances insight.

CHRYSOPRASE

Opaque, apple-green; a member of the chalcedony quartz family. Nickel appears as a trace mineral, thereby producing its green colour. Often found in chunks with brown matrix rock.

Chakra: Heart

Chrysoprase helps alleviate anxiety and apprehension with the unknown. It assists in focusing the mind on the present moment, and helps you see personal problems clearly.

This stone is calming, balancing and healing on all levels. It provides a sense of continuity as you move forward into the unknown. Bolsters self-esteem and enhances communication. Balances energies, male and female, positive and negative, and helps maintain equilibrium.

CITRINE

Yellow quartz. Often citrines are heat-treated amethyst with tell-tale reddish streaks. Natural colours range from lemon-yellow to smoky gold (and it sometimes looks similar to amber).

Chakra: Navel or Solar Plexus

Citrine is excellent for tissue regeneration and strengthening the kidneys, colon, liver, gall bladder, digestive organs and heart. It is a detoxifier.

Citrine raises self-esteem and helps you synthesise your understanding when you feel you are being pulled in many directions. Helpful for mental clarity in communication, writing and problem solving. Enhances optimism and intellectual capacity, creativity and personal power. It holds the energy of wealth. Use for clearing the aura, back problems, cleansing and stabilising the physical body. Balances the thyroid and activates the thymus gland.

CORAL

An organic gem material consisting of calcified skeletons of coral polyps. These tiny primitive organisms attach themselves to previous coral growth and secrete a substance which is similar to calcite through their bases.

Chakra: According to coral colour.

White Coral: Throat Chakra

Strengthens self-esteem and assists with clear judgment; eases frustration and resentment at being told what to do. Encourages you to affirm yourself and recognise the self within. Enhances intuition and calms the emotions. Aligns the chakras and connects you to your etheric body.

Red Coral: Base, Navel and Solar Plexus Chakra

Helps resolve conflict and clear the paralysis experienced due to the fear of making a move. Encourages distance from problems in order to think more clearly about them. Brings you into harmony with the natural environment. Assists in easing indigestion.

CROCOITE

Transparent, red-orange colour. Very delicate, forming crystalline spears and clusters.

Chakra: Navel

Its dazzling, brilliant orange makes crocoite one of the most highly evolved minerals of the orange ray. The energies of crocoite are not subtle, so use as a last resort when working on the navel chakra. It is not a good choice for people new to crystal energies. In fact, its colour serves almost as a warning signal.

Crocoite has a purging effect which may result in nausea if used without careful guidance. On the other hand, when used carefully, crocoite will calm an upset stomach, ease indigestion (what is it that you can't swallow about yourself?), and allow the underlying issues to come through very quickly.

It is excellent in ongoing past-life work, particularly in uncovering Karmic patterns. Provides the strength of character needed to forgive and love those who have harmed you. Use for disorders of the reproductive system and to maintain emotional and mental health.

CUPRITE

Appears as black or deep, transparent, red crystals.

Chakras: Can be used on all chakras but resonates closest with the Base/Root and Heart.

Cuprite enhances the flow of energy throughout the body and balances the subtle bodies. It opens the heart chakra. Excellent for oxygenation of the blood. Enhances self-expression, especially of positive emotional feelings. Beneficial to many organs, especially the blood, heart, brain and bones, and enhances the immune system and central nervous system. Grounding and energising.

DANBURITE

Clear, yellowy and pinkish, chisel-shaped crystals.

Chakras: All. Pink at the Heart.

Danburite enhances psychic ability and otherworld/otherplane connections. Stimulates the intellect, memory and brain. It is joyful, happy, and promotes laughter. Encourages a calm self-assuredness and openness to the world. Excellent for use for disorders of the cardiovascular system, gall bladder and toxaemia. Generally useful for removing toxins from the body and as a protector against pollution.

DIAMOND

Diamond is pure carbon, extremely clear, and the hardest substance known.

Chakras: All, particularly Crown and Third Eye.

Diamond purifies the will, enhances the courage to act on your convictions, and encourages honesty. It is a master healer which dispels negativity and purifies the physical and etheric bodies. Enhances purity and faithfulness; attracts abundance. Encourages you to live by a code of ethics.

A highly spiritual stone which will accelerate the spiritual development of those who wear it. Will repair holes in the aura. Balancing and stabilising.

DIOPSIDE

Diopside is light to dark green, and also occurs in black which, when polished en cabochon, shows a cat's eye or star. It is therefore sometimes referred to as Black Star.

Chakra: Green for Heart, black for Base.

Diopside assists you to remain detached and objective. It stimulates the intellect and clears blocked emotions.

Black Star

During the times of Atlantis and Lemuria, Black Star was used as a scrying stone, so it will take you into the depths. It provides a great deal of protection for those exploring deep spiritual paths, and will keep you connected to the earth while travelling the universe. Provides a direct link to otherworld entities. Excellent for exploring past lives, taking you back slowly and carefully.

Black Star will absorb excess energies which clutter the mind. An excellent grounding stone for those undertaking astral travel. A time link to the past in this life also, and especially helpful for those wishing to resolve childhood trauma and reclaim the inner child. Beneficial for those recovering from incest and abuse memories. Will help uncover early blocks that make you forget.

It can be used in combination with green barite for purging unwanted entities that are almost beings in themselves. Black Star will provide the protective shield, while green barite will dig out that which is not needed and is slowing your development. Use Black Star for problems with the feet which are preventing you moving along life's path.

When a decision needs to be made, consult Black Star. Stare into its shining surface and see the star within which is you.

Green (or Chrome) Diopside

A willing and excellent partner for Black Star. While Black Star resonates with the base chakra and grounds, green diopside heals the heart. Once again, use in healing childhood trauma; green diopside imparts a soothing green ray and heals the emotions that surface when Black Star uncovers them.

In past-life work green diopside will heal the wounds of violent and abusive relationships where you have been in the victim role. It will help you learn how to forgive those who have harmed you in the past, both in past lives and this current incarnation.

Green diopside works mainly on the emotional level, without the astral and interplanetary properties of Black Star. A faceted green diopside will most easily spread the healing green ray, and only a tiny stone is needed.

DIOPTASE

Emerald-green crystalline masses on host rock, often with calcite and sometimes with chrysocolla.

Chakras: All, but especially the Heart.

Dioptase brings a heightened state of awareness and emotional stability. Promotes spiritual development and psychic/telepathic ability. Raises consciousness. One of the most highly spiritual stones.

As an elixir, use dioptase for pains such as headaches and migraines. It can be programmed for use with affirmations that enhance self-esteem and self-worth. Aligns the physical and etheric bodies. Excellent for cellular regeneration and healing.

EMERALD

A brilliant, green member of the beryl family.

Chakra: Solar Plexus, Heart, Third Eye.

Emerald strengthens the heart, liver, kidneys, the immune system and the nervous system. It is a tonic for mind/body/spirit. Enhances dreams and meditation, prosperity, love, kindness, balance, healing and patience. Its energies are uplifting and healing. Helps you recognise abundance in forms other than monetary, and encourages gratitude. Opens and stimulates the heart chakra, calms the emotions. Aids memory and insight. Excellent for past-life work. Eliminates negativity and assists you in attaining a meditative state.

EPIDOTE

Found in deep-green clusters and singly and doubly terminated crystals. Sometimes looks like green tourmaline.

Chakra: Heart and Base/Root.

The main purpose of epidote is to enhance your spiritual path. For those already undertaking the path of spirituality, it will act as a catalyst for going deeper. A very versatile stone.

Place an epidote cluster in a room to spread the healing energy of the heart. Excellent for clearing the atmosphere after an argument. Good for easing tension in offices and other workplaces. Calms and soothes emotions, and restores balance. Use it as a band-aid or bandage for healing recent emotional wounds. Epidote, however, will not allow these wounds to be buried, but will provide a calming effect to enable you to better deal with issues in the future.

Used at the base/root chakra, epidote's energies will ground you to Mother Earth, and when using Australian stones, to the Dreamtime Spirit, taking you to a place of unconditional love and peace.

Epidote enhances your relationship with nature, especially animals, and enables you to better appreciate the natural environment. It is an excellent stone for city people who need to escape to the country. Imparts a feeling of love and contentment with your surroundings. Rest assured that whatever epidote flushes out will be within your coping abilities.

ERYTHRITE

A brilliant pink/red mineral which looks like a velvety covering on its host rock. Also known as cobalt bloom.

Chakra: Heart

Although it appears soft and furry, erythrite is hard-hitting, bursting through emotional blocks and opening the heart.

Erythrite teaches self-love and love of others. It speeds up the path to self-love and self-acceptance. There is no messing around with erythrite. It won't allow you to sit back and wait for things to happen. Rest assured that working along with your Higher Self, erythrite will guide you along your spiritual path.

FLUORITE

Fluorite comes in a variety of colours including violet, blue, yellow, pink, green and clear. Often found in octahedra, but also as a rock and in crystal clusters.

Chakra: According to stone colour.

Fluorite strengthens teeth and bones, improves absorption of nutrients, benefits the blood vessels and the spleen. It is a powerful healer, and helps you grasp more abstract concepts, and develop the ability to comprehend. Balances the positive and negative aspects of the mind. Fluorite enables the mind to maintain a meditative and centred space while in the midst of physical activity. Facilitates interdimensional communication. Generally stabilising and calming. Promotes intuition and understanding.

Clear Fluorite: Third Eye and Crown Chakras

Helps you focus your attention on the present moment and free yourself from the hold of the past. Assists in clearing the mind during meditation. Hold clear fluorite before working with other tools from which you seek guidance (such as tarot or pendulums). Aligns the chakras.

Purple Fluorite: Third Eye Chakra

Is also excellent for meditation, and prepares you by calming the mind and taking you to higher levels of awareness. Its energies are calming and peaceful. Provides clarity and concentration to busy minds. Excellent for students as a study aid, especially for those learning complex subjects such as science and medicine. Enhances rationality.

Green Fluorite: Heart or Third Eye Chakra

Imparts a feeling of oneness with the natural environment - enhances your love of nature. Another stone for clarity, especially on matters concerning relationships (romantic or otherwise) and spirituality.

Yellow Fluorite

Stabilising, particularly in groups where there is conflict. An excellent stone for use in workplaces and at meetings to maintain a calming energy. Balancing on all levels.

A Word About Chinese Fluorite

Chinese fluorite has traditionally been used as a stone of protection and so, regardless of its colour, it will provide an element of protection to those who use it. We have noticed that since the events in Tiananmen Square, many of our Chinese fluorite slabs have been breaking up. We leave the reasons for this to your imagination.

FOSSILS

Fossils hold within them many memories of the past, and are therefore excellent for bringing forward past memories, from this life or past lives. Using fossils for crystal healing or meditation will enhance your ability for past-life recall and will assist in understanding these past influences.

Fossils also represent moving from the old to the new, and are excellent tools for transformation, transition and spiritual development.

GARNET

Garnet comes in a variety of colours, but the best known is the transparent, deep-red, gemstone variety.

Chakra: Root or Heart

Garnet enhances bodily systems, especially the bloodstream, and it stimulates blood flow. Aligns subtle bodies. Love, compassion. Enhances imagination. Garnet can provide a sense of grounding in times of change and upheaval. It will help you feel less depleted at the completion of tasks. Stimulates Kundalini energy and enhances the flow of Kundalini from the base to the crown chakras. Promotes balance and a calming effect when everything seems chaotic.

Green Grossular Garnet: Heart Chakra

Enhances fertility. Promotes cooperation and communal efforts.

GEM SILICA

Quartz-infused chrysocolla which often exhibits areas of malachite and/or azurite.

Chakra: Throat and Third Eye.

Gem silica powerfully imparts the ability to clearly see and verbalise your experience of the world. It is a master stone which carries Spirit in the form of a dazzling aqua light. It is more highly evolved than the blue ray stones, and carries the aqua ray which has not yet been utilised on this planet. However, it is able to be used by us in place of the blue ray, its cousin, at the throat and also at the third eye.

'I am pure spirit,' gem silica says. 'I will assist you in transforming your reality on all levels. I will assist you in advancing spiritually, mentally and emotionally, strengthening you. I will help you on your transition from darkness to light by supporting you and providing you with the love you need to explore, find and change yourself. I am nurturing, but I also encourage much work. When you are blocked, I will break through the barrier and create a path for you to walk. When you have doubts, I will clear away your negativity and enable you to see the way forward clearly and with certainty.'

Gem silica beneficially influences the thyroid, vocal chords, eyes and brain. It is an excellent stone for those passing over as it will ease their transition.

HANKSITE

A waxy-looking, dull, yellowish-grey in the form of tabular and prismatic crystals.

Chakras: All Chakras from the Heart down.

A strong and powerful energy for use in meditation. Hanksite will assist in bringing astral travellers back to their body. Use it under the pillow to assist in remembering dreams and journeys. Hanksite's powerful energy also works on the physical body, and it resonates closest with the heart and lungs. It will assist in calming panic associated with heart attacks. Soothing to the emotions. Helps slow down the metabolism, so it is useful for people with a hyperactive thyroid. Also generally useful as a grounding stone. Works well with hematite.

HEMATITE

Occurs in tabular and rhomboid crystals, masses, plate-like layers and botryoidal shapes. Grey to black with a metallic lustre.

Chakra: Base

Hematite is excellent for mental attunement. It can be used in meditation for connecting to the earth energies. Balancing, grounding, but also energising. Strengthens physical and etheric bodies. Enhances tranquillity and emotional clarity.

Hematite can be helpful for disorders of the blood, nervous complaints and healing broken bones. Assists circulation.

HERKIMER DIAMOND

Small, clear, quartz crystals, usually doubly or triply terminated. Found in the Herkimer area of New York State, USA.

Chakras: All

Herkimer Diamond enhances perception and assists in remembering dreams. Also enhances dreams and helps with easing insomnia.

These brilliant crystals stimulate clairvoyant and psychic abilities and assist telepathic communication. A bridge with past lives. They alleviate tension and calm the mind. Excellent for meditation.

HOWLITE

Most often found in white nodules, but also as masses and tabular crystals.

Chakras: Heart, Crown

Howlite can help to deepen sleep, and assist you in remembering dreams. It is excellent for insomnia. Soothes the heart. Assists memory, and eases pain, stress and anger; promotes tactfulness. Excellent for bone disorders caused by calcium deficiency as it helps the body maintain calcium levels. Therefore howlite is also good for the teeth.

IOLITE

Iolite is the gem trade name for translucent blue and violet cordierite. It is a magnesium aluminium silicate.

Chakra: Third Eye or Crown

A direct link to your soul. Iolite assists in understanding why you are here and helps channel healing energy. Connecting with your soul through iolite brings a total state of unconditional love. Imparts a feeling of protection as you receive the energy you need. Strengthens and aligns the aura with the subtle bodies. Balances male and female energies. Strengthens all aspects of the physical body.

JADE (Green)

Jadeite and nephrite, both called jade by the gem trade, have similar characteristics - both have a monoclinic crystalline structure. Jadeite is rarer and is a sodium aluminium silicate.

Chakra: Solar Plexus, Heart

Promotes the practice of detachment from the emotional body. Encourages selective, focused thought.

Jade has a focused, calm balance. Excellent in past-life and dream-work. Provides balance for those who are emotionally over-sensitive.

Jade can be used to assist clear judgment and for preparing for meditation. It resonates strongly with the heart, kidneys and immune system. Dispels negativity. A sacred stone to many primitive peoples.

Nephrite (New Zealand)

Nephrite best corresponds to the heart chakra. It is a good companion stone for rose quartz, kunzite and rhodochrosite. When used in body layouts it will work very well with lapis, as nephrite is a great but unrecognised power stone. Its energies are softer than its dark appearance would suggest. It is a gentle healer.

Use this stone if you are undergoing surgery, as it will help to calm your nerves. It is good to place a piece of nephrite under the pillow to enhance deep and restful sleep.

Nephrite transmutes anger into acceptance and assists in forgiving those who would hurt you. Provides a gentle but firm barrier of protection for sensitive people in tense, noisy and negative vibrations and energies.

When used as a meditation stone, hold nephrite in the left hand and direct the stone's energy to the heart chakra. It will assist you in decision-making concerning spiritual and emotional matters. A very valuable stone for those starting out on the path of spiritual development. Nephrite has the potential to become a very good friend.

JASPER

Usually considered a variety of chalcedony, some people place jasper as a group within itself in the quartz family. It is found in all colours.

Chakra: According to stone colour.

All jaspers can be used for aligning the chakras and promoting physical well-being. An excellent physical healer, regardless of colour.

Picture Jasper

The picture jasper discussed here is the yellow to yellow-brown variety with swirls of creams, gold and orange. It is no accident that picture jasper has chosen its name, for it is an excellent companion tool for use in creative visualisation.

If you have a visual block and trouble clearly seeing what you want or need, hold picture jasper in your left hand and contemplate its surface. For example, if it's travel that you want, imagine its swirling surface as a map of all the places you would like to go. Tread every path and build upon the picture you already visualise. Imagine the face of a person you would like to see and speak to them from the heart. See your essence engraved upon the surface of the stone and imagine yourself doing whatever you like to do. Needless to say, picture jasper will assist you in meditation for solving problems and deeper thinking. Excellent for use in creative visualisation.

Yellow Jasper: Solar Plexus Chakra

The deep, golden yellows of this stone resonate closely with the solar plexus. Use yellow jasper for easing feelings of powerlessness and emotional blocks at this chakra. Eases the pain of ulcers and indigestion (when something is eating away at you). Calms and soothes a nervous stomach. Enhances the whole of the digestive system. A powerful physical healer.

Red Jasper: Base Chakra

Soothes menstrual pain and helps clear pre-menstrual tension. For men, it is an excellent healer for prostate problems. A good grounding stone. Beneficial to the reproductive organs, blood system and bladder.

Green Jasper: Heart Chakra

Very quickly helps to open the heart chakra and clear blocked energies, enabling you to express yourself more effectively. Use in combination with a throat stone such as turquoise or celestite, for assisting in expressing the heart's desire. An excellent stone for healing the heart, lungs and upper digestive organs.

Rainbow Jasper: Root, Navel and Solar Plexus Chakras
Combines the energies of red and yellow jasper, with an added bonus of aligning and clearing all of the lower chakras.

Indian Jasper: Base or Navel Chakras
A swirling composite of yellow/tan and brown jaspers, forming tiny, intricate patterns on the stone. Indian Jasper will assist you to find your path in life. It has strong oracular properties.

Irai Jasper: Base/Root or Heart Chakras
Irai Jasper comes from Irai, Brazil, and is a composite of red and dark-green jaspers. Occasionally all red or all green stones may be found. The predominantly red stones work more closely with the base chakra, the green with the heart. Bi-coloured stones are suitable for the whole lower chakra area from the heart down.
Helps to clear blocked energies. Assists in warding off negative vibrations and energies. Provides comfort in times of stress. Grounding and stabilising to the emotional and mental bodies. Excellent to carry around for general protection, but particularly for situations where you need to be in control of your mental and emotional states. One of the strongest physical healers of all the jaspers.

KUNZITE
A variety of spodumene. Pink, green, pale yellow and clear crystals are found. Green kunzite is also known as hiddenite.
Chakra: According to stone colour.

Kunzite is beneficial to people with addictive behaviours. It strengthens the cardiovascular system and aids manic depression. Generally a good balancer on all levels. Enhances self-esteem, tolerance and acceptance. Soothing, calming. Expresses emotional equilibrium; enables the inner dimensions of the heart to be experienced. A powerful personal meditation stone. Kunzite helps to balance negative emotional states. It assists you to attain a deep meditative state.

Pink Kunzite: Heart Chakra
Accelerates your creative potential and the desire to express that potential. Increases enthusiasm and zest for life. Helps speed up spiritual growth.

Clear Kunzite: Third Eye Chakra
More active than pink kunzite and more focused on understanding creativity in the spiritual realm. Ask it about timing in the pursuit of your activities.

Green Kunzite (Hiddenite): Heart Chakra
Stimulates the intellect and promotes insight and understanding. Connects us to other worlds.

KYANITE
Translucent blue or blue-green aluminium silicate. A metamorphic rock. Colour is often in irregular streaks.
Chakra: Crown, Third Eye, Throat.
Kyanite strengthens the throat chakra. The life-force energy of kyanite can open the way for spiritual healing. It facilitates astral/ interdimensional travel; enhances creative expression. Opens the third eye, and is particularly useful on this chakra during meditation, especially if you are having difficulty in relaxing and clearing the mind. Transforms negative thought patterns. Opens up the

crown chakra to assist in contacting your Higher Self. Good for dream recall and enhancing sleep. Kyanite also helps you understand your dreams. Promotes clarity and understanding. Calming, tranquillising.

LABRADORITE

An opaque, grey stone that shimmers with blue and green iridescence. A member of the feldspar family. It is found in the Malagasy Republic as a labradorite-moonstone, clear with brilliant blue highlights. Also known as Spectrolite.

Chakra: Third Eye and Crown in particular, but can be worn anywhere on the body with equally good effect.

Labradorite will answer your questions about your spiritual purpose. Utilise it for accessing the Akashic Records. It accelerates telepathic abilities and assists communication with your Higher Self. Helps balance and stabilise the movement of the Kundalini. An excellent meditation stone.

In ancient Scandinavia, labradorite was used as an oracle by the indigenous peoples, and it can be beneficially utilised in a similar fashion in this age. This stone will connect you to the elements - wearing it in the sea, for example, will enhance your connection to water energies. Labradorite will benefit the nerves, brain, pineal and pituitary glands and lymphatic system.

LAPIS LAZULI

Deep (royal) blue with spots of white and/or gold. The white flecks are often calcite, the gold are tiny spots of pyrite.

Chakra: Third Eye

One of the power stones of the ages. Lapis Lazuli serves as both a mental and spiritual cleanser. It strengthens the skeletal system. Activates the thyroid gland. Releases tension and anxiety. Enhances strength and vitality. Facilitates the opening of chakras. Assists creative expression.

Lapis Lazuli helps you look at things you have been avoiding, and can help you become aware of reasons why you are ill. Excellent for past-life work. Connects the physical to the astral plane and promotes spiritual growth and psychic ability. Expands awareness and enhances the ability to take in more of what is going on around you. Eases depression. Balances male and female energies.

LARIMAR

Gem-quality blue pectolite. Its beautiful blue comes from traces of copper.

Chakra: Throat

Larimar is useful as a confidence builder, especially when spiritual changes are taking place. It helps you move out of conventional ways of thinking. Excellent for brainstorming. Assists in using power and knowledge wisely, particularly in spiritual matters. Helps lighten depression. Imparts calmness, serenity and purity. Beneficial to the spleen, thyroid, lymphatic system, muscles and nerves. Brings in the feminine energies of the blue ray and imparts the Goddess energies.

LEPIDOLITE

Appears in the form of masses, mica-like layers and tabular crystals. Often found with spears of pink tourmaline.

Chakra: Heart

Because of its high lithium content, lepidolite is excellent for those with addictive behaviours, manic depression and chronic depression. It alleviates stress, anger and internalised self-hatred. It promotes a smooth transition when you need to make changes in your life. Opens the heart to promote self-love and love of others. Calming and soothing. Relieves stress and tension in the physical environment. Excellent for use in classrooms and workplaces.

LODESTONE (Magnetite)

A metallic, black iron oxide. Its distinguishing feature is its magnetic property.

Chakra: All, but especially the Root.

Lodestone helps draw out and alleviate illness and pain from the physical body. It assists in the release of emotional trauma. Increases resistance to stress and disease. Gently but firmly propels you towards change. If you are reluctant and fearful of leaving behind old ways, lodestone eases these fears and helps you grow. Gives protection when you are around people, or in a place which imparts feelings of depression or agitation. Its energy is clearing and building.

When you are utilising lodestone in body layouts, it is best to place it next to the body, rather than directly on the chakra, to avoid the body absorbing too much of its energies which can be toxic if overused. Likewise, when handling lodestone, hold it in a tissue.

MALACHITE

A layered, green, opaque stone. It is a copper carbonate, hence its intense green colour. Often found with other copper-based minerals such as azurite and chrysocolla. Will lose its sheen if soaked in salt water - cleanse by smudging with sandalwood or sage incense.

Chakra: Solar Plexus, Heart

This stone helps you take the initial step in uprooting fear by assisting in understanding its source. Intense and probing. Helps you break free from limitations; increases courage and determination as it dissolves fear and anxiety. Assists in the release of old, limiting patterns. Vitalising for body and mind. Draws out pain from injuries. A balancer on all levels. Influences the pancreas and spleen.

Aids tissue regeneration.

MARCASITE

The marcasite discussed here is a tumble-polished Australian stone which is black with streaks of marcasite appearing as goldish swirls.

Chakra: Crown or Base/Root

Use at the crown chakra for bringing in the Light. Despite its mostly dark colour, the golden threads are reminiscent of the cord that links the spirit to the body in astral travel. When used as a meditation stone, it will offer you protection from any surrounding negative vibrations.

Hold marcasite in your left hand and feel the stone's energy rising up your arm to the heart, then up through the throat and third eye to the crown.

Marcasite is a good stone to carry with you to job interviews or meetings with bureaucrats employed in government departments. The stone will help surround you with a protective field and leave you feeling calmer and more able to express yourself.

It is also useful at the base chakra for connecting to the earth energies. In this respect it is similar to hematite, but with a much gentler feeling. Excellent for city dwellers who are bombarded with noise and grime on a daily basis. Marcasite helps you cope. Beneficial to the brain, eyes, heart and circulatory system. Builds immunity.

MICA

Mica forms in plate-like layers, scales, masses and tabular crystals. Colours range from grey, brown and yellow to greens, reds and purples.

Chakra: According to colour.

Star Mica: Solar Plexus Chakra.

The clusters discussed here are yellow/gold. They are highly energising, especially for the physical body. Spreads healing energy very quickly and will do the job of rutilated quartz if it is unavailable. One problem with star mica is its tendency to crumble. However, just imagine little platelets of healing energy falling where needed! Star mica is excellent for developing the intellect and academics could well use a piece in their classrooms. It also brings an equilibrium to the emotions. Use it as an elixir for appetite suppression.

MOLDAVITE
A green, glassy tektite material found only in Czechoslovakia.

Chakras: Heart and Third Eye

Moldavite is a mysterious stone, about which debates have been raging. Is it a stone which fell to earth, or is it the result of a meteorite hitting the earth? In any event, it is clear that moldavite's energies have much to do with space and extra-terrestrials.

Some people believe that moldavite has been placed on this world specifically to assist the Star Children in acclimatising to life in a physical body on the planet. However, moldavite has been shown to assist people to make extra-terrestrial contact. It opens the heart chakra and will often be a catalyst for sudden and important changes in your life, particularly on an emotional level. Moldavite also opens the third eye and helps deepen insight during meditation. An excellent stone to use for facilitating astral travel and communication with spirit guides.

MOONSTONE
A translucent, milky stone, which occurs in yellow, peach, grey, colourless and blue. A potassium aluminium silicate variety of feldspar.

Chakra: According to stone colour.

Moonstone generally assists with emotional release; it provides the key to maintaining balance and wellness on all levels. It has a calm, flowing peace that helps restore emotional balance in everyday experiences. Excellent for understanding dreams about your emotional state; also assists in sensitive response to the emotional state of others.

Blue/Grey: Heart Chakra
Healing to the stomach, spleen and pancreas. Relieves anxiety and stress. Emotional balancer and soother which is helpful for anyone who is over-emotional. Enhances flexible attitudes.

Blue/grey moonstone is useful for women during menstruation to balance hormonal and emotional activity. It helps men to become more in tune with their feminine aspect.

Orange/Peach: Navel or Solar Plexus Chakra
Softens the ego, allows more vulnerability, enhances the giving capacity and creative interpersonal relationships. Relieves stress. Enhances self-confidence, warmth and nurturing. Influences the ovaries, spleen, womb, colon and bladder.

MORGANITE
A pink member of the beryl family.
Chakra: Heart
Morganite has a soft, soothing energy to ease emotional pain, trauma and depression. It is an excellent stone to heal the pain of separation in relationships. Softens anger and calms an over-emotional state such as hysteria. Transmutes fear and anger into positive healing energy. Helps remember past trauma and assists in releasing buried memories and pain. Morganite has a feminine energy which is nurturing, stabilising and caring.

OBSIDIAN
Obsidian is a natural volcanic glass, most often found in black or snowflake (black with white inclusions which look like

snowflakes). Also found in varieties of green, aqua-blue and mahogany.

Chakra: According to colour of stone.

Black (Apache Tears): Root/Base Chakra
One of the most important teachers of the New Age stones. Influences the stomach and intestines. Connects mind and emotions. Grounds spiritual energy. Helps clear subconscious blocks. Powerful healer for those attuned with it.

Black obsidian offers a doorway to your inner depths. It is powerful and intense but very nurturing. Only use it when you are educated about its powers and prepared to process the changes that the stone will put you through.

When using black obsidian in healing, it is a good idea to have a clear quartz in close proximity as it will polarise the intensity of black obsidian and help dissolve and neutralise any physical or emotional debris that surfaces. Helps in eliminating toxins from the body.

Snowflake: Root/Base Chakra
A lighter approach to exploring your inner depths. The black and white colour communicates the balance of polarities: dark - light, male - female, yin - yang.

Green: Heart Chakra
Also known as Mount St. Helen stone. Green obsidian resonates most closely with the heart chakra. It is a much less demanding stone than black obsidian and is particularly useful in personal meditation for exploring the inner self.

Mahogany: Root/Base or Solar Plexus Chakra
Provides continuity in energy flow. Helps release anger and activates a positive sense of power.

ONYX

A variety of chalcedony.

Chakra: According to stone colour.

Onyx is generally a good stone to use as an emotional balancer and to relieve stress and tension. It assists in creativity and inspiration. Strengthens bone marrow.

OPAL

A member of the quartz family. Colours can be white, grey or black background, with flashes of blue, green, orange, red and yellow.

Chakra: Third Eye and Crown but can be used on others.

Opal will work well with the emotional, mental, spiritual and etheric bodies. Its focus is to clear and build. It can provide you with a much-needed burst of energy, especially when you are lacking self-confidence. Excellent for enhancing creativity and intuition, releasing anger and enhancing feelings of self-worth. Helps connect you to your Higher Self.

PEACOCK ORE

Found in rock form with a metallic lustre that ranges from yellow, green, blue, red and purple. Also known as chalcopyrite.

Chakras: All

Use peacock ore/chalcopyrite for calling in the colour rays of the upper chakras, from the solar plexus to the crown, during meditation. Its blue, green and violet sparkling surface will reflect in turn, depending on your needs. It will ground the colour rays into the physical body, providing a bathing effect, rather like taking a bath in soothing blue waters. Aids concentration, particularly when there is learning to be done.

Peacock ore/chalcopyrite is a good stone for clearing the mind of excess energies and calming jumbled thoughts. Beneficial to the brain, pineal and pituitary glands.

PERIDOT

Also known as olivine. Colours range from yellow-green to olive green. A magnesium iron silicate.

Chakras: Heart or Solar Plexus

Enhances a feeling of inner joy and lightness. Opens you to giving and receiving and expressing this joy. Builds confidence and a feeling of oneness with the world. Accelerates personal growth. Resonates well with the heart, pancreas, spleen and liver. Reduces stress. Aids tissue regeneration.

PRASE

Green member of the quartz family, found often with brown markings from its matrix rock.

Chakra: Heart

Prase links the root and navel chakras to the heart. It is especially useful for resolving issues of sexuality and easing sexual guilt. Beneficial to the reproductive and sexual organs.

Prase is an excellent stone for women undergoing abortions, to help resolve guilt and feelings of loss. Also useful for soothing the emotions following miscarriage or stillbirth. Prase will teach that the lost life has chosen its own destiny.

Australian prase enhances the dream state and provides a sense of oneness with the universe. A very loving and caring stone.

PREHNITE

Yellow-green, pale green, brown-yellow.

Chakras: Heart, Solar Plexus

Prehnite is an excellent stone for meditation and relaxation. It balances and enhances the flow of energy along the chakras. Often used as a relationship stone, to enhance the bonding of personal relationships. Clears the mind for clarity of thought and expression. Beneficial to the brain, nerves, bones and cardio-vascular system.

PYRITE

A brassy, silver to gold-coloured iron mineral which occurs in clusters, chunks, cubes, and more rarely as flat, circular plates often called 'suns' or 'sand dollars'.

Chakras: All

Pyrite assists with concentration and memory. It is an excellent stone for students and others who need to remember new information.

It is also excellent for developing spiritual vision and psychic ability, and is a good companion for amethyst in this regard as it will help ground spiritual/psychic understanding and imprint it on your cellular memory.

Pyrite resonates with the energies of the sun and is joyous and uplifting. Use at the third eye for the purposes of spiritual/psychic development. Use at the solar plexus for the purpose of enhancing personal and psychic power and to transmit thought-forms to another or to the universe. Pyrite can be used at the base chakra and crown chakra simultaneously to open the chakras to channel and to ground the information received. Can also be used in combination with fluorite and calcite as part of the Mental Trinity for learning and understanding. Influences the eyes, brain and bloodstream.

QUARTZ CRYSTAL (Clear)

A silicon dioxide. Also found with a milky or cloudy appearance.

Chakras: All

Quartz crystals reflect pure white light that can be channelled into daily thoughts, feelings, words and actions. By touching, wearing, using or meditating with these crystals, you can work with that light in a physical form.

They enhance the crystalline properties of blood, body and mind. Emotional balancer, dispels negativity. Stimulates brain functions. Receives, activates, stores, transforms, transmits and amplifies energy and thought forms. Excellent for meditation. The most easily programmed of all crystals and healing stones because of its crystal shape and flat faceted sides and points, and the most useful of healing stones.

A cluster of quartz crystals in a room can transmit healing energies. Use clear quartz crystals for contacting your guides and for interdimensional communication.

Beneficial to the whole body, but especially the pineal and pituitary glands.

REALGAR (and Orpiment)

Orange, massive mineral with shades of brilliant red, orange and iridescent yellow/gold.

Chakra: Solar Plexus

When you are feeling powerless to make changes, realgar will swiftly cut through blocked energies at the solar plexus. Incredibly joyful and uplifting - a very powerful stone that must be used with a grounding stone such as hematite, black tourmaline or smoky quartz.

Promotes inter-dimensional communication and connects you with spirit guides.

The purpose of realgar is to assist in enhancing your understanding of what you want in your life and what you must sweep away or tone down. Use realgar in meditation held at or laid upon the solar plexus. It assists with forgiving and releasing past actions. Links the energies of the heart chakra to the navel and base chakras, releasing blocks that prevent the occurrence of healing.

RED QUARTZ

The stones discussed here are the doubly-terminated red quartz crystals from Valencia in Spain, however the properties also apply to other red quartz crystals.

Chakra: Base

Red quartz cuts through negativity like a sharp knife. It dispels pessimism and generally helps build a happy, joyous and positive attitude towards life.

Helps you enjoy life as it is. Dissipates greed, jealousy and envy and helps you to be satisfied with what you have. Very good grounding qualities.

Red quartz helps to align the chakras from the base chakra up, and will help ground light and healing energy into the physical body. A very under-estimated crystal.

RHODOCHROSITE

Rose red, pink with white stripes

Chakra: Heart

Beneficial to the spleen, kidneys, heart, pituitary gland and circulatory system. Emotional balancer.

Use rhodochrosite when healing emotional wounds and soothing trauma. An excellent companion to rose quartz and pink kunzite at the heart chakra. Resonates with the subtle bodies. A very powerful healing stone.

RHODONITE

Red or pink with black inclusions of manganese oxide.

Chakra: Heart

A very calming and soothing stone. Beneficial to the nervous system, thyroid, pituitary gland and pancreas.

Rhodonite can be used for improving your reflexes. It strengthens immunity and memory. Good to use for both physical and emotional trauma. Builds confidence and self-esteem. Increases energy levels.

Meditate with rhodonite when you feel you need time out from a hectic and stressful life.

ROSE QUARTZ

A pink variety of quartz, rarely found in crystal form, usually as rocks. Its colour ranges from milky, pale pink to a deep, lavender pink.

Chakra: Heart

Dynamic intensity and healing power. A healer for internal wounds. Aids the kidneys and circulatory system. Increases fertility. Helps clear stored anger, resentment, guilt, fear and jealousy. Reduces stress and tension, cools tempers. Enhances self-confidence and creativity.

Rose quartz promotes love, forgiveness and compassion. It is often called the 'love stone'. When healing with or wearing rose quartz, be prepared for emotional releases and the surfacing of suppressed memories and feelings.

RUBY

Varying red colours; a member of the corundum group. Found in hexagonal crystals or discs, sometimes rhomboidal.

Chakra: Base/Root or Heart

Ruby is excellent for revitalising the bloodstream, circulatory system, and generally for balancing the body's operations. Strengthens immunity. Imparts a sense of strength when dealing with difficult situations, and enhances your belief in yourself. Energising, particularly when you are feeling sluggish or drained.

RUTILATED QUARTZ

Quartz crystal with inclusions of the mineral rutile, which look like fine needles of silver or gold colour.

Chakras: All

Assists regeneration of tissue. Enhances the life force. Strengthens the immune system. Eases depression, facilitates inspiration. Enhances communication with the Higher Self. Rutilated quartz is a very powerful healer. It will move healing energy quicker along the physical chakras than clear quartz, and will enhance the healing energies of all other stones. When you are feeling negative, use rutilated quartz to enhance your belief in yourself.

SAPPHIRE

Various shades of blue, but also colourless, pink, yellow, green, purple and black. Blackjacks are sapphires that have become too dark to use as gemstones in jewellery. The varieties discussed here are blue sapphire and blackjack.

Chakra: According to stone colour.

Blue Sapphire: Throat or Third-Eye Chakra - use the lighter ones at the Throat and darker at the Third Eye.

Blue sapphire assists the entire glandular system as well as the heart and kidneys. It enhances psychic abilities and assists in bringing clarity to scattered thoughts and ideas. Use sapphire to connect to your spirit guides and teachers, and for interdimensional communication. Connects body, mind and spirit, and assists in connecting to your Higher Self. An intensely spiritual stone. Enhances creativity.

Blackjack: Base/Root Chakra - use blackjacks for grounding.

A good partner with blue sapphire during meditation to keep you grounded while contacting guides and extra-terrestrials. Assists in pulling the spirit back to the body when astral travelling. Highly energised, happy and joyful stones.

SCAPOLITE

A yellow, pink, violet or colourless crystal that closely resembles kunzite. Also known as wernerite.

Chakra: Crown, Solar Plexus.

Use scapolite at the crown chakra for bringing in the Light. It will bathe you with golden light, and heal all of the upper chakras.

At the solar plexus it will assist the free flow of energy through the whole chakra system, especially when there is a blockage at the solar plexus. Scapolite helps you deal with current losses such as the death of a loved one. It will also assist with the manifestation of money when times seem desperate.

Scapolite can be used for drawing out muscular pain, particularly around the lower back and stomach. It helps release tight muscles. Scapolite contains messages for those who come across it, and is useful for past-life healing when those lives are causing emotional blocks in the present. It resonates closest with the sun energies, and can best be cleansed in this fashion. Beneficial to the heart, lungs, muscular system and brain. Works mostly on the emotional level, where emotional wounds and blocks are manifesting as dis-ease and pain. A stone that will come into its own towards the end of the decade.

SELENITE

A variety of gypsum. Occurs in long, striated, translucent wands, yellowish clusters, shining white clusters that resemble fishtails, and rose-like clusters (desert rose).
Chakras: All, but particularly the crown.

Selenite assists in grounding white light into the physical body. It can be used for cleansing and clearing auras, clearing negative energies from objects, people and rooms, and for cleansing other crystals. Strong protective qualities. An excellent meditation stone in all its forms. Aids concentration and clarity.

SMITHSONITE

Light blue, light green, yellowish, pink and lavender. Often looks like bubbles on matrix rock.
Chakra: According to stone colour.

A stone to assist in remembering and understanding dreams. Softens the emotions. Promotes spiritual growth and understanding. Brings tranquillity to stressful situations; soothing and calming.

Smithsonite assists in physical healing, particularly of flesh wounds. Beneficial to the sexual organs, reproductive system, metabolism and bloodstream.

SMOKY QUARTZ

A variety of quartz crystal. Its colour ranges from deep black through browns and yellowy browns. Be careful of some very dark or black smoky quartz crystals as they have often been irradiated and their energies have died.

Chakra: Root/Base

The energy of smoky quartz will initiate movement of the primal forces of the body. It strengthens the adrenals, kidneys and pancreas. Increases fertility and balances sexual energy. Aids depression. Mildly sedative and relaxing. Grounding and centering. Excellent for meditation. Enhances dream awareness. A good stone to use for people who manifest suicidal feelings, depression, fatigue or feel spaced out.

Morello Smoky Quartz (Victoria)

These small smoky quartz crystals have a shape similar to Herkimer Diamonds and, indeed, could be known as Australian Herkimers.

A Morello smoky crystal can be used to help remember and interpret dreams. Also good for concentration because of its grounding qualities; it prevents you from being too flighty and losing yourself in daydreams, especially when bored. Helps stimulate the intellect and converts gut feelings into clear thoughts. An active healer, Morello smoky will assist on the physical and emotional as well as mental levels.

Morello smoky quartz helps with the feet - sprains, cuts and bruises - which prevent you from walking forward in the physical sense. At the same time, problems with the feet indicate a block on some other level, manifested in the physical.

Morello smoky quartz crystals have been under-estimated. As well as their own particular qualities, they also encompass the general qualities of smoky quartz.

SODALITE
A bright blue stone, often crisscrossed with white and grey lines.

Chakra: Throat or Third Eye

Sodalite aids the pancreas and strengthens metabolism. Alleviates fear. Calms and clears the mind. Slightly sedative, grounding, brings clarity, enhances communication and creative expression. It helps clear old mental patterns from the subconscious to make way for conscious thinking. The white lines and flecks symbolise the spiritual light that comes with a balanced mind.

STAUROLITE (Fairy Cross)
An orthorhombic crystal which is most often found as crystal twins forming a cross.

Chakra: Root/Base

Grounding, linking you to Mother Earth. Creates a bond between humans and the natural environment, and is therefore good to use with epidote. The cross formation signifies the meeting of spirit and matter, death and rebirth, and so it is with our leaving our past behind as we move on to our spiritual destiny. It will help heal the break between our past and future lifestyles.

Staurolite shows that the transition from darkness into light is easier than we think. It encourages a less materially-based existence. Helps manifest that which is needed to make our physical lives comfortable and assists in rejecting that which does not benefit us spiritually. At those points where our spiritual life must meet with our material existence, staurolite smoothes over the cracks and aligns all levels of our Being so we can feel more comfortable in our Selves.

STRAWBERRY QUARTZ

A rare, pink quartz which occurs naturally as part of a total crystal, but sometimes with terminations.

Chakra: Heart

A link between the physical and subtle bodies. Excellent for past-life recall and contacting the 'source' or 'spirit'. A very strong healing energy vibrates through this stone - stronger than rose quartz. It is said that strawberry quartz was used in Atlantis and Lemuria in healing ceremonies and to stimulate recall of the 'beginning'; it was held by the high council, those being the most spiritually developed of the realm.

This is not a beginner's stone, but will accelerate the development of those already on their spiritual path. Also good to ease tension in relationships, particularly when one party chooses not to understand the growth or changes in the other.

SUGILITE

A purple stone. Also known as luvulite or royal azel.

Chakra: Third Eye or Crown.

This stone has only surfaced in the last decade. Its purple ray represents the link between the mind and the physical body. Enhances pituitary and adrenal glands. Strengthens the heart. Aids physical healing and purification. Emotional balancer, reduces stress. Excellent for meditation. One of the best stones to be used by sensitive and open people.

SULPHUR

Crystalline or massive in formation in bright yellow,

honey-yellow, brown-yellow, light green or red-yellow. The crystals discussed here are bright yellow clusters.

Chakra: Solar Plexus

Sulphur enhances your ability to stay focused without stray thoughts distracting and intervening. It is excellent for use in study and other endeavours where concentration must be at its optimum. Dispels negative energies. Utilise sulphur as a companion in process work, particularly in releasing old patterns. Do not wash sulphur to cleanse, smudge it with sage or sandalwood.

SUNSTONE

A member of the feldspar family. Also known as aventurine feldspar. An orange-brown stone with a metallic glitter.

Chakra: Navel

Sunstone helps you move forward when you are feeling blocked on life's path. It encourages exploration of your possibilities in life. Removes the feeling of being limited in potential. Primarily used for spiritual expansion.

TEKTITE

The tektites discussed here are the black, glassy nodules found in Central Australia.

Chakras: All, but especially Base.

This is a helper stone for moldavite. These black tektites provide a more grounding energy. Use them between the feet and at the base chakra while meditating with moldavite.

Each tektite is like a world unto itself. Stare at its surface and see caverns, hills, mountains and lakes. Tektite will take you anywhere you wish, but will always bring you back. Highly energising. Good for people with addictions to sugar, food and alcohol. A tektite will remind you of the sweetness in life.

Get to know your stone, for it will give you information that you will find most useful as you journey.

TIGER EYE

A golden-brown chatoyant stone, a variety of quartz.

Chakra: Solar Plexus

Tiger eye benefits the spleen and pancreas, digestive organs and colon. It is an emotional balancer, grounding, centering, softens stubornness. Builds a firm foundation for spiritual expansion. Enhances personal power.

TIGER IRON

A composite of tiger eye, red jasper and hematite.

Chakras: Solar Plexus, Navel, Base/Root.

Tiger iron will powerfully impart the energies and properties of all three of its composite stones. In addition it will enhance creativity, particularly in spiritual pursuits.

It is an excellent stone for meditation for writers and artists who utilise a spiritual dimension in their work. Rejuvenates the blood and circulatory system. Very good for those with low immunity. Promotes the swift healing of infected wounds. Excellent to use for healing dis-eases such as herpes, chicken pox, shingles and cold sores. Definitely a stone for motivation on all levels: career, relationships, getting what you want and need.

TOPAZ

Found in blue, clear and golden crystals. Gold topaz is also called imperial topaz.

Chakra: According to stone colour.

Topaz is excellent for tissue regeneration. It is an emotional balancer, cooling, soothing, peaceful and tranquil. Enhances understanding, creativity and self-expression. Use gold topaz at the solar plexus or crown, blue at the throat, and clear on any chakra.

Clear Topaz

This stone is uplifting. It assists understanding, especially in studying and reading.

Yellow/Gold Topaz

Helps assimilate new knowledge to use for practical application. In combination with citrine, it is an excellent stone for students and researchers.

Blue Topaz

Similar to clear topaz, but with a calmer and more soothing energy.

Smoky Topaz: Base Chakra

Grounding and stabilising; this is one of the stones which can be used during astral travel to come home comfortably to the physical body. Smoky topaz works on all levels, so it can also be used very much for physical grounding during times of stress such as job interviews, to assist in clear thinking and concentration. Also calms emotional upset and upheaval. Helps you maintain equilibrium when all around seems chaotic and unstable.

TOURMALINE

Tourmaline comes in many colours. Blue and blue-green tourmalines are known as indicolite; pink and red as rubellite; green and red is called watermelon tourmaline; black is also called schorl, and brown-black is known as dravite. There are also green, lavender, clear and yellow varieties.

Chakra: According to stone colour.

Tourmaline is a powerful healing stone. It dispels fear and negative influences and has strong protective qualities.

Green Tourmaline: Heart Chakra

Clears emotional pain and confusion. Soothes worries and

calms anxiety. Balances emotional highs and lows. Regenerative and rejuvenating. Use green tourmaline wands in body layouts, as the striated crystal structure will assist the flow of energy through the chakra system. Beneficial to the pituitary gland, nervous system, larynx, thyroid gland and lungs.

Pink/Red Tourmaline (Rubellite): Heart Chakra

Promotes a detached acceptance. It has a more energetic and uplifting energy than green tourmaline. Opens the heart to joy. Enhances perception and insight. Releases fear, guilt, grief and sorrow. Beneficial to the immune system, heart, circulation, nerves and endocrine system.

Watermelon (Green/Pink) Tourmaline: Heart Chakra

The combination of pink and green tourmaline means that watermelon tourmaline combines the best of both worlds. Use it in situations where either green or pink tourmaline is needed. Helps balance conflicting male and female energies. Strong protective influence.

Blue Tourmaline (Indicolite): Throat and Third Eye Chakras

Helps in decision making when you are feeling in conflict about which path to take. Teaches you to value your intuition. Focuses personal power and helps you point it in the right direction. Enhances clairvoyance. Strengthens the nervous system.

Black Tourmaline (Schorl): Base Chakra

Grounding. A very down-to-earth stone which speaks the truth and assists you to do likewise.

Black tourmaline helps you keep your feet on the ground in both the physical and metaphysical sense. It is one of the most commonly used grounding stones for crystal healers (it works so well).

If you have a tendency to feel light-headed when working with crystals and other energies, a piece of black tourmaline in your hand, pocket, or between your feet will help you remain grounded. Protects against negative energies; it will deflect these energies back to their source.

Black tourmaline has far-reaching memory. It is excellent for assisting in bringing up memories hidden deep inside you. Works very much on a cellular level. Can take you back to the times of Atlantis and Lemuria, gradually bringing you back through past lives and present reality, clearing and releasing negative thought patterns as you go and at their first occurrence.

This crystal will help in long-term work, by providing a stability that may seem lacking in your past. It is excellent for people whose lives are unstable, for example, people who constantly travel, change relationships, or whose environment is changing around them.

TURQUOISE

Opaque sky-blue to blue-green or apple-green stone. Most often found in matrix with veins of limonite, sandstone, jasper, and sometimes with malachite or chrysocolla.

Chakra: Heart or Throat

Turquoise is excellent for tissue regeneration and for toning and strengthening the physical body. It enhances awareness of the interconnectedness of life, and one's connection to the mineral, plant or animal kingdoms. Encourages self-expression, especially when used at the throat chakra. Promotes emotional balance and peace of mind. Aids the circulatory and respiratory systems.

UNAKITE

A composite of orange/pink feldspar, epidote and quartz which occurs in massive form.

Chakra: Heart, Solar Plexus

Unakite balances the heart and is a good stone for people who are givers but not takers. It enhances self-esteem and feelings of self-worth, and enables you to accept love and caring from others. Unakite also enhances your sense of personal power, and strengthens the solar plexus chakra.

It encourages you to be more forthright about your needs and desires, and to go ahead more confidently and get what you want in life. Transmutes feelings of worthlessness to worthiness, self-hatred to self-love, self-doubt to confidence and belief in your power and ability.

Unakite is a stone of transformation from negativity to positivity. It promotes a feeling of oneness with the natural environment.

Appendix I
The Seven Physical Chakras

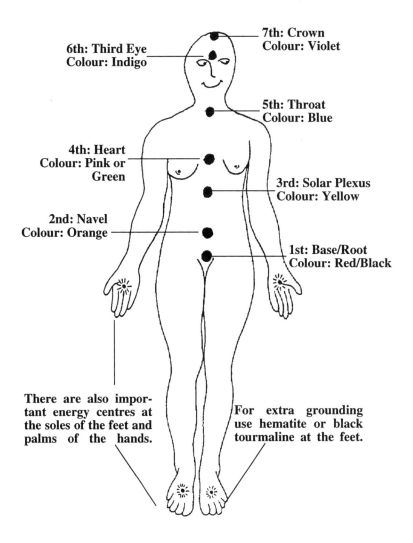

6th: Third Eye
Colour: Indigo

7th: Crown
Colour: Violet

5th: Throat
Colour: Blue

4th: Heart
Colour: Pink or
Green

3rd: Solar Plexus
Colour: Yellow

2nd: Navel
Colour: Orange

1st: Base/Root
Colour: Red/Black

There are also important energy centres at the soles of the feet and palms of the hands.

For extra grounding use hematite or black tourmaline at the feet.

Appendix II
Chakras and Corresponding Stones

Base or Root (1st) Chakra

Agate - Crazy Lace
Agate - Fire
Agate - Dendritic
Aragonite - dark brown
Barite - brown
Bloodstone
Boji Stone
Calcite - red
Cassiterite
Coral - red
Cuprite
Danburite
Diopside - Black Star
Epidote
Garnet
Hematite
Herkimer Diamond
Jasper - red
Jasper - rainbow
Jasper - Indian
Jasper - Irai
Lodestone
Marcasite
Obsidian - black or apache tear
Obsidian - snowflake
Obsidian - mahogany
Onyx - black
Peacock Ore
Pyrite
Quartz Crystal
Red Quartz
Ruby
Rutilated Quartz
Sapphire - Blackjack
Smoky Quartz
Staurolite (Fairy Cross)
Tektite
Tiger Iron
Topaz - smoky
Tourmaline - black (Schorl)

Navel or Sexual (2nd) Chakra

Agate - Dendritic
Amber
Aragonite - red/brown
Boji Stone
Calcite - red
Calcite - gold
Carnelian - red or orange
Chalcedony - white
Chiastolite
Citrine
Coral - red
Crocoite
Danburite
Herkimer Diamond
Jasper - Rainbow
Jasper - Indian
Moonstone - orange/peach
Peacock Ore
Pyrite
Rutilated Quartz
Sunstone
Tiger Iron

Solar Plexus (3rd) Chakra

Amber
Ametrine
Aragonite - gold/yellow
Aventurine - peach
Boji Stone
Calcite - honey
Calcite - red
Carnelian - yellow
Chalcedony - white
Citrine
Coral - red
Danburite
Emerald
Fluorite - yellow
Herkimer Diamond
Jade - green
Jasper - picture
Jasper - yellow
Jasper - rainbow
Malachite
Mica - golden star
Moonstone - orange/peach
Obsidian - mahogany
Peacock Ore
Peridot
Prehnite
Pyrite
Quartz Crystal
Realgar (Orpiment)
Rutilated Quartz
Scapolite
Smithsonite - yellow
Sulphur
Tiger Eye
Tiger Iron
Topaz - golden/Imperial
Unakite

Heart (4th) Chakra

Agate - Botswana
Agate - Moss
Apatite - Yellow and Yellow/Green
Apophyllite - Green
Aragonite - white or cream
Aventurine - green
Barite - green
Bloodstone
Boji Stone
Calcite - green
Calcite - pink and peach
Chrysocolla

Heart (4th) Chakra (Contd.)
Chrysoprase
Cuprite
Danburite (especially pink)
Diopside - green
Dioptase
Emerald
Epidote
Erythrite
Fluorite - green
Garnet
Hanksite
Herkimer Diamond
Jade
Jasper - green
Jasper - Irai
Kunzite -pink or green
Lepidolite
Malachite
Moldavite
Moonstone - blue/grey
Morganite
Obsidian - green
Peacock Ore
Peridot
Prase
Prehnite
Pyrite
Quartz Crystal
Rhodochrosite
Rhodonite
Rose Quartz
Ruby
Rutilated Quartz
Smithsonite - lavender and pink
Strawberry Quartz
Tourmaline - green
Tourmaline - pink (rubellite)
Tourmaline - watermelon
Unakite

Throat (5th) Chakra
Amazonite
Angelite
Apatite - blue
Aquamarine
Blue Lace Agate
Boji Stone
Calcite - blue
Celestite - blue
Chrysocolla
Coral - white
Danburite
Gem Silica
Hanksite
Herkimer Diamond
Kyanite
Larimar
Peacock Ore
Pyrite
Quartz Crystal
Rutilated Quartz
Sapphire - blue
Smithsonite - blue/green
Sodalite
Topaz - blue
Tourmaline - blue (Indico-lite)
Turquoise

Third Eye (6th) Chakra
Amethyst
Ametrine
Aragonite - purplish colours
Aventurine - blue
Azurite
Azurite/malachite combination
Boji Stone
Celestite - blue or clear
Charoite
Chrysocolla
Danburite
Diamond
Emerald
Fluorite - clear
Fluorite - purple/blue
Fluorite - green
Gem Silica
Hanksite
Herkimer Diamond
Howlite
Iolite
Kunzite - clear
Kyanite
Labradorite (Spectrolite)
Lapis Lazuli
Moldavite
Opal
Peacock Ore
Pyrite
Quartz Crystal
Rutilated Quartz
Sapphire - blue
Smithsonite - blue
Sodalite
Sugilite

Crown (7th) Chakra
Agate - Tree
Alexandrite
Amethyst
Ametrine
Apophyllite - Clear
Boji Stone
Calcite - gold
Calcite - Icelandic (clear)
Calcite - Stellar Beam
Celestite - clear
Cerussite
Danburite
Diamond
Fluorite - clear
Hanksite
Herkimer Diamond
Howlite
Iolite
Kyanite
Labradorite (Spectrolite)
Marcasite
Opal
Peacock Ore
Pyrite
Quartz Crystal
Rutilated Quartz
Scapolite
Selenite
Sugilite
Topaz - clear

Appendix III
Bibliography

A short list of useful books about crystals and healing stones.

The Women's Book of Healing by Diane Stein, Llewellyn Publications USA, 1988.
Looks at working with crystals and gemstones, auras and laying on of hands, chakras and colours. A feminist book, useful for women and men.

Michael's Gemstone Dictionary by Judithann H. David and J.P. Van Hulle, Affinity Press, USA, 1990.
A compendium of channelled information (through Michael) on crystals and gemstones.

Love is in the Earth: A Kaleidoscope of Crystals (Volume 1) by Melody, Earth Love Publishing House, USA, 1991.
A reference book describing the metaphysical properties of the mineral kingdom. (Volume 2 of *Love is in the Earth* deals predominantly with layouts.)

The Newcastle Guide to Healing with Gemstones by Pamela Louise Chase and Jonathan Pawlik, Newcastle Publishing, USA, 1989.
A guide to using over 70 different gemstone energies.

The Newcastle Guide to Healing with Crystals by Pamela Louise Chase and Jonathan Pawlik, Newcastle Publishing, USA, 1989.
A guide to balancing the human energy system with quartz crystals.

Crystal Enlightenment (Volume 1)
Crystal Healing (Volume 2) and
The Crystalline Transmission (Volume 3) by Katrina Raphael, Aurora Press, USA.
A combination of channelled information on crystals and gemstones and some practical ways of using stones (My favourite books!)

Practical Guide to Crystal Healing by Marc James and Dhyan Klein, Gemcraft Books, Australia, 1988.
An inexpensive and easy-to-follow beginner's guide to crystal healing by two Australian authors.

The Crystal Healing Book by DaEl Walker, The Crystal Company, USA, 1988.
A guide to using crystals for healing and personal growth. Includes simple techniques for pain reduction, balancing, relieving symptoms and colour healing.

Crystal Wisdom by Dolfyn, Earthspirit Inc., USA, 1989.
A comprehensive guide to the spiritual and healing potential of crystals and gemstones.

Appendix IV
Resources

Sheril Berkovitch - Labrys
433 Brunswick Street, Fitzroy Vic. 3065
☎ (03) 417 7388
Basic crystal workshops; short workshops for groups, using crystals as an oracle.

Trisha Ellis - The Crystal Academy
PO Box 289, Daw Park SA 5041
☎ (08) 293 3447
Introductory through to intensive practitioners courses. Private healing sessions, workshops and seminars. Trisha is also a Reiki Master/Teacher and Pranic Healer.

Nadine Perry
☎ (03) 523 8161
Workshops on crystals, colour and sound. Other workshops are also available.

Pam Arnold - Crystal Affinity
315 Keilor Road, North Essendon Vic. 3041
☎ (03) 379 5678
Crystal workshops are conducted at Pam's shop.

Barbara Buchanan - Trias Healing Centre
PO Box 139, Moreland Vic. 3058
From introductory to intensive crystal courses.

Lynette Forrest - Belgrave Crystal and Reiki Centre
PO Box 136, Belgrave Vic. 3160
☎ (03) 754 5982
Introductory to practitioners courses. Private healing sessions. Reiki Master. Women's mystery facilitator.